break free ᴄ.
significant quantity discounts, wᴎᴇ..,
bulk for client gifts, sales promotions, and
premiums. Special editions, including books with
corporate logos, customized covers, and letters
from the company or CEO printed in the front
matter, as well as excerpts, can also be created in
large quantities for special needs.
For details and discount information for both print
and ebook formats, contact the author Paige
Johnson-Serjue by email
breakfreeofthebs@gmail.com or at
https://breakfreeofthebsbook.com

Paige Johnson-Serjue
www.paige1ofsome.com
Cover Designer: Ryan Pornasdoro

Published by "Fairy Godmother" Debbie Horovitch of Social Sparkle & Shine
Social Sparkle & Shine is a legacy and storyteller's publisher, creating even more authority for accomplished individuals, with highest quality book publishing and thought leadership in media channels (strategic publicity). For a free assessment of your own publishing and bestseller potential, email Debbie Horovitch at debbie.horovitch@gmail.com Visit our website at www.DebbieHorovitch.com

Library and Archive Canada Cataloging-in-Publications Data:
ISBN-13: 978-1-77316-033-7
ISBN-13: 978-1-77316-034-4 (ebk.)

Published in Canada

FIRST EDITION

book 1 of some

are you ready to get bullsh*t free?

break free of the

bullsh*t

A Millennial Empowerment Guide

Paige Johnson-Serjue

<u>Dedication</u>

Another dedication page directed to someone else that you probably don't know.. Not today. This one's for YOU!

And to some people you may not know (but are equally amazing):

To the love of my life, Ajay, our son Jacob and our unforgettable Angel

To my parents, sister Aliah and Grandpa Young

And to the universe - thank you. It isn't close to enough but you say I talk too much anyway.. ☺

Love you forever

Cool Things People Said

Life changing and highly recommended!
Regardless of your age or point in life you can learn something from this book!
It's direct, personal and forces you to take action!
- *a.j. s*

This book brings a modern touch to life and cleanses your way of thinking!
It's completely motivating and highly recommended if you're trying to reach your goals - pulls you right out of procrastination and slaps you with storytelling strategies!
- *adrian r*

Engaging, interactive and a motivating read. I couldn't put it down! 5 stars!
- *aliah j*

This book is beyond amazing, relatable on so many levels!
We all experience self doubt and this book will definitely free you from that.
I wish this book came out years ago because the exercises really helped me reflect on my past and how to take the right steps to breaking free of the bullshit.
- *cyndi a*

The reality check you've been waiting for!
-   *debbie y*

I'm fortunate to know Paige and this book is a testament to all that she stands for.
I wholeheartedly believe we're meant to create a vision greater than ourselves. Paige will propel you on that necessary journey and then some.
-   *ghazala k*

Amazing positive energy!
We've all been in a funk like this before and this is exactly what people need to hear!
Love how it's interactive with the reader and gets us putting pen to paper which is something we all lack sometimes and is a great way to set yourself up for success!
Thank you for sharing your struggles and how you've been able to find the inner motivation to the "no more bullshit" attitude to turn things around and be the motivation to us through this amazing book!
-   *j.c c*

This book re-establishes what it takes to be successful in our ever changing world.

Through a deep dive into personal accountability, this honest read allows everyone to dive into and break down barriers surrounding personal achievement.

- *joey s*

Eye opening and challenges your mind and way of thinking for the better!

- *jordan s*

I had to grow up very fast compared to most of my "friends" so I don't necessarily fit in with the description of the typical millennial yet, when you were explaining some of the roadblocks or the "crap" we deal with today - I related on a level that I wasn't expecting!
And the activities presented, especially after a lesson is really enticing to a reader TO TAKE ACTION. It's one of the best qualities about this book, and there are A LOT of great qualities.
If you need daily motivation, READ THIS BOOK. If you need guidance, READ THIS BOOK, a kick in the butt? READ THIS BOOK!

- *josh b*

Inspiring !
A great book for anyone who needs tips on new ways to look at life. A lot of helpful tips to live your best life and most positive life !

I loved every second of it. It's the kind of book that you may revisit often when you need a dose of motivation, and a reminder for self love!

- julie p

An absolute must read!

Not only is it a page turner but the exercises included are a huge bonus (really had me motivated and thinking positive towards future goals).

Reading this book opened my eyes to so many surrounding factors that can cause you to create excuses, bring yourself down and stop you from achieving your goals.

If you feel you're stuck and need that extra push to get you motivated then READ THIS DAMN BOOK!

The author shares personal stories of failure which really allows you to connect and relate to your own stories. She also discusses starting your own business. "The hardest thing to do is START, and that is successful itself" — this quote directly from the book and I couldn't agree more. Oftentimes, we think we haven't accomplished anything by just starting, but we're wrong ! Starting is probably the most important part of your success story!

All in all, I read this book twice because I enjoyed it that much and I'll probably reread it again! Definitely a 5/5 star rating!

- *marlena m*

Paige's technique and approach isn't your everyday narrative. She hits us with her own truth along with mini exercises to self reflect.

After reading "Break Free of the Bullshit," I was convinced that whatever I had left pending to do, would get completed much sooner as the only thing stopping me was myself.

Highly recommended for anyone at any age to read this book as self sabotage is a hump we all need to push through!

- *schenelle d*

CONTENTS

If Not You, Then Who?!

*"this book will make a difference in your
life as long as you're willing to let it"*

We can all revisit a time in our lives (or you're currently in it) where you wanted to make something happen for yourself. It's almost like an 'ah-ha' moment, that makes you sooo excited to the point of you skipping all the steps needed to get you there; and you're already envisioning your future. Maybe it was a new job, starting a business, becoming a better person, learning something new, saving money, getting healthy, anything… but it doesn't matter what it was because you didn't do it!

You're not alone. We often come face to face with the fear of failure, self doubt, judgment from our peers, comparisons on social media and a million other imaginary factors that we give priority to. Priorities that convince us of being incapable of doing something that we are born to do. I should have written this book four years ago, but I was in a constant battle with my own self and always let the bullshit excuses win.

Until now.

As you continue this reading experience I will be the empowering voice in your head that breaks away at the negativity and self-doubt. **This book will make a difference in your life as long as you're willing to let it.**

Now, you may be one of those people that delays making a change unless it's a monumental day so *Happy New Year, Happy Birthday, it's the first of the month, happy Monday..* whatever day you need it to be it is today, because it is time to

Break Free of the Bullshit!

01

What is the Bullshit?

"you picked up this book to make a change, there is evidently some form of bullshit YOU want to break free from"

It is important to outline the *'bullshit'* that you are about
to permanently remove from your life.

The bullshit is anything or anyone that can or is holding
you back from fully being empowered in your personal
and/or professional life. It ranges from your surroundings,
your thought process and your own personality.
Essentially, it is a pile of excuses you make for yourself
and the people around you that allows you to feel content
about being mediocre. You might be familiar with some of
the below statements:

"I'm not ready to start."

"It isn't my time yet."

"I'm too busy."

"I'm lazy."

"I don't know enough about the industry yet."

"Too many people have done it already."

"No one will support me."

If one of these thoughts have crossed your mind at any point, then I am extremely happy because you're in the right place *(insert happy dance here)*! That bullshit mentality is what we are en route to removing!

Step 1: Take a moment to choose one goal that you've been meaning to accomplish but haven't. This can be personal (ie. Self love, fitness, sociability etc.) or professional (entrepreneurship, growth in current company, educational etc.):

<u>*Step 1.2*</u>*: Now it's time to really analyze yourself and your surroundings! List the specific bullshit that is responsible for the excuses of you not attaining this goal:*

This is a necessary step in creating your purpose. **This book is not intended to be another self-help product that you can post on social media to imply that you're bettering yourself without actively taking the necessary steps.** You picked up this book to make a change, there is evidently some form of bullshit YOU want to break free from and if you don't want to do the work then there's your answer for *step 1.2.*

You're welcome.

02

Defining Empowerment

"once you become empowered, no one can tell you shit"

According to Oxford Languages, empowerment is defined as *"the process of becoming stronger and more confident, especially in controlling one's life and claiming one's rights."* Essentially, **once you become empowered, no one can tell you shit.** The act of being empowered though is a mental action that YOU must commit to. YOU have to take ownership of who YOU are and what YOU'RE doing. YOU also need to trust yourself, love what YOU do and embrace imperfect moments.

This is much easier said than done. It's bad enough that the narrative around our generation is commonly negative. We are constantly being surrounded by images of an "*avocado toast eating, broke, hyper-sensitive youngster that would rather live in their parents' basement forever so they can backpack through Europe.*" On top of that, social media constantly depicts everyone '*living their best lives*' without struggle. Telling us how to look and what we should be doing. How can we love who we are, trust ourselves and embrace imperfections when we're surrounded by a lifetime supply of bullshit!?

You do it by breaking free of it!

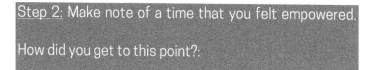

Step 2: Make note of a time that you felt empowered.

How did you get to this point?:

I was en route to getting kicked out of University in my third year. Shit was hitting the fan and I had to take a step back and be vulnerable with myself.

How did I get to this point!?

When did the snowballing occur!?

I needed to love myself enough to want to be in better situations, understand my '*why*' so I could work towards my goals, trust that I can make it happen and realize that everything didn't have to be perfect.

Walking across that stage to receive my degree was one of the most empowering experiences I have ever had. To know that I could bring myself out of SUCH a low point - not just mentally, but financially and emotionally shaped my life indefinitely!

We need to do what we can to find empowerment in all circumstances, whether it's a monumental change or learning experience. Remember who the hell you are and come out on top.

YOU got this!

03

You're the Problem and the Solution

"you are the only person in control and are fully capable of making shit happen for yourself"

When something doesn't work in our favour we're so quick to blame anyone, anything or anyplace.

Have you ever thought you could be what is standing in your way?

Obviously this isn't always the case.. but it was for me.

When I was about to get kicked out of University, I was convinced the system was against me. *High school didn't set me up for success, my friends were holding me back, my job was giving me too many hours, my parents were putting pressure on me..* anything you could think of, I thought it.

But I was full of shit.

I was too scared to take responsibility for my own actions! Even though I knew I had exams to study for and essays to write, I knowingly allowed everything to snowball. You'd think when I got that first warning, I'd make a change.. Nope. I deflected, acted like it never happened and hoped something would randomly work in my favour.

I remember visiting my parents for the holidays and told them I was getting 80s in my courses but I was actually being called into the Dean's Office for plagiarism.

After accepting my bad grades wouldn't magically reverse, I finally decided to take the necessary steps and ask for help and stop worrying about keeping up that fake *'perfect image'*.

One of my peers suggested I speak to the Academic Advisor that was in charge of my electives *(the only thing I was excelling in and what I should have gone to school for in the first place – Media and Communications)*. I went to Brock University, a fairly large institution in terms of number of students so I automatically assumed I would be treated like a number and brushed to the side to count down the days until the school kicked me out. I was already at rock bottom so another layer of disappointment wouldn't hurt..

I couldn't have been more wrong.

Penni Lafleur, *Academic Advisor for Communications, Popular Culture and Film* is her title at the University. Therapist, academic advisor, cheerleader, accountability partner and life saver seems more fitting in my opinion. Penni helped me *'break free of the bullshit'* in a way that forced me to take responsibility for my faults but also understand that I can still come out on top.

Our first meeting was the first time I spoke honestly about where I went wrong and I was embarrassed, vulnerable and eager to stop the bullshit but didn't know

the first step. She immediately provided that safe space

and blueprint to success.

She was blunt yet compassionate. Helped me yet held me

accountable. All in all, she is one of the top 3 *bullshit free*

people I've ever met and I am beyond thankful. With her

guidance, I worked my ass off and only had to stay in

school for an additional year AND graduated with honours.

Sometimes we need someone on the outside to help us

understand what we're truly capable of.

I wouldn't change that experience for the world because

it made me into the person I am today. It was proof that

I was toxic to myself but overcame that and was empowered to see what I was truly capable of.

Almost failing University is not the most common story, but talking negatively about ourselves and downplaying your talents is. We are responsible for taking ourselves to the next step – whether it's growing in your job, starting your own business, getting healthier, being a better person etc. We've been conditioned to think that speaking highly of ourselves or talents is associated with bragging. It's NOT and we need to end that narrative. When we speak highly of ourselves, people will think the same. If you're downplaying your talents – how do you expect people to take you seriously?

When I spoke at my first event I was approached by a potential customer questioning my cost. I responded with, *"I'm not that experienced so I'm not charging yet."* In that moment I not only spoke negatively about myself and talents but I diminished all interest that this potential client had in me. Do you think I got booked? Nope!

When you're unhappy with yourself or you're holding onto negative aspects of the past, you start projecting that on other people and self sabotaging situations. You're not only toxic to yourself but to those around you. You need to address the bullshit then let that shit go, because it is 100% holding you back! You can't keep making excuses or playing the blame game when shit doesn't work out for you, especially when **you are the** only person in control and are fully capable of making

shit happen for yourself.

<u>Step 3</u>: It's time to take ownership so we know what we

need to work on! What are your toxic traits?:

<u>Step 3.2</u>: What are your positive traits?:

We all have toxic traits but we need to ensure we are holding ourselves accountable. Once you are aware of what is negative you become further awakened to these traits that are holding you back.

04

Quarantine and Chill?

"you can build to become the best version of yourself but also spend days laying around doing nothing"

"WTF, we're living through a pandemic?!"

This was one of the countless WTF's that went through my head. There was also the *"WTF will happen to my job, my sons' daycare and the health of my loved ones and I?"* Then, like most people I was laid off - this was an entirely new level of *WTF's*. The thought of our bills, my son's education and how long we can survive with our savings haunted me daily.

If you were on social media during this time the tone gradually progressed from *"yay, no work!" (for most of us)* to *"bored in the house and I'm in the house bored" (TikTok)*, to *"if you aren't taking this time to start a successful business, build your dream body and become the best version of yourself then you're not shit!"*

Step 4: What emotions were you experiencing at the peak of Covid-19?:

I want you to make note of your emotions because they were not something that was a main point of conversation. If you do not discuss how you're feeling about something, how can you properly react or solve an issue!? Now think about why you were feeling those things.

Were you scared for your health or scared because you didn't take the steps to be financially literate and prepare for something like this?

Were you sad because you have to distance yourself from friends and family or sad because you made excuses to not see them in the past when you know you should have?

Maybe it is all of the above.

Prior to Covid-19 I was working more than 40 hours a week, had limited family time and when spending time with friends we'd plan expensive outings.

Why?

Because this is what was normal for most of us. This was the culture we lived in because we rarely knew or saw any different.

Depending on when you are reading this book your reality can vary but as of now we are in Stage 3 and my life has taken a complete change within these past five months. I've been able to spend entire days with my family to where we almost reconnect, I'll be going to work soon and a more balanced work schedule has been implemented and when hanging out with friends we are spending time outside and being active. My mental health is stronger overall and I'm genuinely a happier person.

Life with Covid-19 is a time of balance, despite what social media tries to imply. You can build to become the best version of yourself but also spend days laying around doing nothing.

Step 4.2: How has this pandemic changed you?:

The worst thing that can come of this pandemic is if we stay the same.

Coronavirus forced us to realize that our day to day normalities were *'the bullshit'* for the most part and we need to not only adjust those behaviours but also prepare ourselves if it were to happen again.

05

The Power of Social Media

"a lot of us deal with the internal battle of comparison more because we are still trying to find our place in the everyday world, as well as the world of social media"

Remember when social media was social?

I remember going to a friend's birthday and uploading three albums worth of photos because Facebook would only allow 60 at a time. I remember only socializing with people I knew..

I think we underestimated the innocence of what social media once was because I don't think anyone could have predicted its power today.

Being active on some form of social media is common for our generation. It is a convenient way to share your life and opinions as well as an economical way to grow and start your business; *but have you considered the power it has on your sense of self, habits and general outlook on life?*

Aside from the large list of positives, there are countless examples that show how famous social media is for making us feel shitty about ourselves. We went from only communicating with people we know to having *'access'* to the personal lives of celebrities and other influencers constantly displaying all the good things money can buy.

If you are not in their tax bracket and are constantly seeing these images of what you *should* have, how you *should* look etc. – it can be extremely depressing, *don't you think?*

Or can it be a good thing?

In my love and hate battle with social media, I've found that; like most things, it's all about perspective – your attitude towards or way of thinking about something.

Let's use a scenario of a random celebrity, choose your favourite and replace *"Blah Blah"* with their name:

"Blah Blah" has just posted a video on their social media account of their new home, which is comparable in size

to your favourite shopping mall. On top of that, you've lost count of the number of cars and other cool shit they have on their property.

Then you reflect on your life. Your place might be the size of their bathroom and you've only experienced what they have in their backyard at an all-inclusive resort.

How does that make you feel? (there is no wrong answer):

Answer 1: Like shit

Answer 2: Motivated

Answer 3: I don't care

When you are able to *break free from the bullshit* comparisons of social media and adjust to a more empowered mindset, posts like this will either motivate you or not interest you!

It is more common that people will post the best version of themselves or situations on social media in comparison to the bad, so when you're going through a tough time; you're led to believe everyone's life is perfect, and you got the short end of the stick. Once you realize and accept that social media is commonly everyone's *(including celebrities and influencers)* highlight reel – you'll feel a lot better.

Back to the scenario: instead of feeling shitty after a post like that, find the positive and let it motivate you.

This act of motivation boils down to your goals and desires for the future you're trying to build. If a big home and multiple amenities are something you want – use that post as a virtual vision board as something to work towards, research how *"Blah Blah"* got to that point, review the housing market and meet with a financial advisor to get a plan in place so you can attain these goals and be that motivation for someone else!

When we witness things *(material or not)* that we label as *'amazing'* we shouldn't feel like shit about it – it should motivate us to put the steps in place to get to where we want to be.

Now, what is *'amazing'* to you?

This is what the third answer is about. If having a mansion is not something of value to you, the post shouldn't have any effect on you.

There is also something to be said about comparing yourself to someone not because you want what they have but because you don't see what you do have. **A lot of us deal with the internal battle of comparison more because we are still trying to find our place in the everyday world, as well as the world of social media.**

So how do we break free of the bullshit of social media and turn all your perspectives into either positive or nothing at all?

Here are two easy ways:

1. *Unfollow the accounts that do not motivate you, make you want to be better or are not realistic. Let's be real, you can't be positive about everything out there however, if you are constantly seeing negative or unrealistic images daily, it will affect you.*

After having my son I wanted to get in shape. I followed a bunch of fitness accounts for inspiration and workouts but I continued to feel like shit.

Why?

Because I was either following females that did not have a baby, got surgery, or were rich and had a trainer and chef.

2. *Start following accounts that will motivate you and that are in line with your goals and aspirations.*

Same fitness example, I began following *'Mom Bod'* inspiration and workout pages as well as those focused on healthy eating.

And remember, it's not only people you DON'T know that are sucking you into the bullshit – it can be your friends and families accounts as well. **Unfollow them too!**

Step 5: What types of social media accounts will inspire you *(ie. motivational speaking, sports, health etc.)*?:

You also want to keep that same inspirational energy for your own social media accounts!

Step 5.2: How does your social media account inspire others or create a positive space?:

I know <u>for a fact</u> that if **all** users placed importance on what other members could positively gain from engaging with them, there would be A LOT less bullshit to deal with!

06

Failing Properly

"failure is some imaginary shit that we make up in our minds that is most likely NOT going to happen"

What is your experience with failure?

Who told you failure was a negative thing?

Why are you scared to fail?

Putting yourself out there in general is scary but the above were the questions I asked myself in my attempt to challenge my own limiting beliefs when starting my own business.

<u>Step 6</u>: Name 2 experiences where you felt like you failed *(ie. school, business, relationships):*

I've created business ideas in the past that didn't work out the way I had planned and in other cases I wasn't putting in the work that was needed. Whenever these situations occurred *(which was often)* I would deflect and not take ownership in any way possible. After really reflecting on those above questions I progressed to learning to take ownership of my mistakes, understanding my capabilities and adjusting my mindset to **fail properly**.

'Fail properly'. Not something you hear too often..

When shit goes wrong, you can't just let it happen. You do what you can to fix it, you learn from it, find strength in it and you empower others with that story; because you are not the only one that had that experience.

To fail properly is to learn and grow from the experience.

Step 6.2: Based on your answer in *step 6*, reference how you *'failed properly'*:

g up we had countless experiences with failure

that have shaped our minds into the negative narrative

of today. Our friends, family, education system, media

and countless other sources are telling us that *failure is*

bad, don't fail, we don't like failures etc (roll your eyes

with me, please!).

Failure is some imaginary shit that we make up in our

minds that is most likely NOT going to happen but WILL

likely stop us from even starting something that is

potentially amazing. Also, the majority of Millennials use

social media so we're scared of what our peers will think

IF we fail.

We create a million and one reasons as to why we can't accomplish something new before the pen touches the paper to draft the damn idea.

Has this happened to you?

There is no reason why you can't start and there is nothing holding you back from starting except your damn self!

Again *(in case it wasn't clear)*, <u>THERE IS NO REASON WHY YOU CAN'T START!</u>

Why are you allowing yourself to live a mediocre life because of an imaginary circumstance you made up in your head?

Failure should be looked at as a <u>hurdle we want to overcome,</u>

<u>a challenge we want to experience and win in exchange for</u>

<u>personal growth, education and advancement.</u>

If it was easy, everyone would be doing it!

Get out of your own head, get out of your own way and

make shit happen!

07

WTF is Success?

"we are so quick to look at success as an end result and not take note of the successful milestones that bring us to that point"

Step 7: How do you define success?:

Growing up we're always reminded by society, family, friends, the media and our own thoughts that *we have to be successful*. Even if we don't have something specific to attach the word to, *we must be successful*.

We will literally drive ourselves crazy without fully recognizing what success is.

I correlated success to a high income. I assumed if someone had a lot of money, a nice house, maybe a fancy car; they *must* be successful. It's almost impossible not to think that as a teenage Millennial. The majority of cartoons, music videos and reality shows correlated success with financial freedom and other material items.

Now if we fast-forward to today, the idea of numerical success is forced down our throats via social media! All of a sudden you're considered *'successful'* based on the amount of followers you have or likes you get? In turn, we start basing our success off of comparisons of other people and their numbers.

We need to stop that.

We are so quick to look at success as an end result and not take note of the successful milestones that bring us to that point.

The hardest thing to do is START, and that is successful IT SELF!

You're reading this book to *Break Free of the Bullshit* - success.

You ate healthier today - success.

You've accomplished a short or long term goal - success!

Celebrate the small wins!

<u>You're a successful ass person, give yourself some</u>

<u>credit!</u>

There are sooo many elements, levels and situations to

this *'being successful'* shit!

Once you realize that, you'll find it's a lot easier to reach

those long term goals and you'll be an overall happier

person.

Step 7.2: What was the goal you wrote down for step 1?:

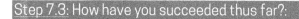

Step 7.3: How have you succeeded thus far?:

Are you aware that you have already made successful moves to your response in step 1?! And here you were thinking you were starting from scratch.. ha!

You're already ahead of the game - be proud of yourself!

I'm proud of you!

08

Getting Lost in *'Love'*

"do not base your wholeness, success and happiness on another person"

I don't think people understand the weight that a potential love interest has on you *Breaking Free of the Bullshit*, because in relationships; most people are full of shit.. including you.

We are now a technology reliant, social media using, virtual gathering, down in the DM's ass generation *(especially during Covid-19)*. Not all of us but YOU DEFINITELY fall in <u>at least</u> three of those categories. Again, nothing wrong with that - this is how society has evolved and the majority of those descriptions work perfectly in a friend, family and/or corporate setting but becomes a big ass strain on a new relationship.

On top of the normality of everyday life:

1. It is common that one or both people in this potential relationship have been hurt before and have their guard up. A guard that they want YOU to break down, even though you *most likely* don't know it exists *(reading that sounds ridiculous I know.. But I've been there and you most likely have too)*.

2. The beginning of the relationship is pretty fake if you aren't already familiar with each other. You're commonly trying to show the better version of yourself.

3. Depending on your age, you want to know what their goals and accomplishments are and if they align with yours, but when you crept their social media it's too hard to tell.

We need to remove the bullshit mentality that we need a significant other to make us whole. All the "*you complete me*" foolishness needs to come to an end. <u>Do not base your wholeness, success and happiness on another person</u>. In the words of a social media post that has been circling around with no credits, *"if they are happy alone, they will be happier together."*

We enter these new relationships with the focus of doing what we can to have the other person like us.

Why?!

You *should* want to be yourself in the beginning so you don't continue to waste your time. On top of that, couples need to **make face-to-face communication a priority** in their relationship. You're hurt, want to talk about the future, need to set guidelines, want to know about each other's day - whatever - you NEED to talk about it because the physical part of your relationship will only take you so far!

I've been with my now husband for well over a decade and we learned the importance of communication very early on due to the beginning of it being long distance. When you are essentially living two different lives *(and in some cases in different time zones)* it is crucial to involve your partner in the moments of your day! This habit continued when we were back in the same city and it is a **major** element that kept us so strong.

With that being said, I also have to address the seasoned couples out there: if your partner for the most part does NOT do the following:

Want you to be better

Uplift you

Celebrate your wins but downplays them

and you have taken the necessary steps to rectify the situation - **LET THEM GO!**

Easier said than done, but you need to start outlining the steps to do so because <u>that negative energy will 100% hold you back.</u> Stop giving yourself excuses and stop holding onto the good times hoping they'll come back. <u>They won't.</u>

It's time to put yourself first.

<u>Step 8:</u> If you are single, what are your 3 non-physical must-haves from your future partner?

Step 8.2: If you are in a relationship that you're happy in, what has kept you both going?

Step 8.3: If you're in an unhappy relationship what is the next step to breaking free from it?

It is important to remind yourself of the *positive attributes* of your relationship because they are so easily forgotten throughout the day to day. Regardless of how long you have been in one - never stop dating, flirt when possible and share your feelings *(good and bad).*

Love isn't always easy but it is a beautiful thing. Ensure that you are experiencing that to its fullest capacity because you deserve it!

09

Breaking the Cycle

"do not let other people's character flaws cripple you"

A large factor of our actions is based on what we've witnessed and experienced as a child. For example, we've commonly heard people say, *"a daughter will look for a partner similar to her father."* But what if your Dad's an asshole? Do you subconsciously date assholes because that is what has been normalized in your life to a point where you don't know any better?

I was judgmental, hurt, combative and lacked a lot of belief in my own self based on my experiences growing up. Don't get me wrong, I was still positive for the most part and had a very open relationship with my immediate family but it was a large portion of my external family that imbedded these negative traits in me.

When I would be confronted about these traits my response would be, *"well that's just the way I am."* It didn't cross my mind to change those behaviors because I didn't notice that they were limiting me.

I knew my family had issues, *but doesnt every family have issues?*

It wasn't until a few months before my wedding that I realized it wasn't good for my mental health to keep using that excuse to defend my relationship with them. Their negative, judgemental and self consumptive traits that were trying to overshadow one of the most important days of my life well before it even happened was a whole new level of bullshit that I had to break free from.

I made the decision to love this group of family members from a distance and cut ties.

"But Paige.. That's your family! Blood is thicker than water! Just deal with it!"

I've heard it all before and completely understand where anyone is coming from because I was preaching these same words.

The narrative of accepting toxic behaviours from family members *(and anyone for that matter)* into your everyday life and routine is wrong.

I spent decades defending ridiculous behaviour because these behaviours were normalized.

A couple months after my wedding I found out I was pregnant. The thought of my child not meeting these family members crossed my mind multiple times especially since they were a big part of my childhood *(note: although there was a lot of bullshit in my adult life, I have some amazing memories with them when I was younger)*. I also jumped back and forth with the idea that I could have made a mistake.

I shared my thoughts with my good friend, who's simple response changed the game for me. She said, *"Paige, you may be ok with surrounding yourself with negativity but as a mother you are responsible for the energy you allow around your child."* Deep right? I know.. That comment had me realize that I was not only *breaking free of the bullshit* for myself but also breaking the cycle *(in advance)* for my child.

Regardless of the example, at this age <u>you know right from wrong, good from bad. You have enough common sense to make the necessary changes to be a better person.</u> What's crazy is, we have NOT seen anything positive come from those negative attributes we carry on so WHY do we continue them?

We need to give more time to self reflection, we need to take note of how we act and react to different situations and understand why we do the things we do and feel the way we feel.

It's time to break the cycle.

You're better than those negative examples that were normalized when you were growing up. <u>Do not let other people's character flaws cripple you</u> (*read that again*)!

<u>Step 9</u>: Reflect back to your toxic traits in *step 3*, which of those were embedded in you from your childhood?:

Step 9.2: Describe one thing that you will do to break the

cycle and how it will benefit you:

Wow.. Look at you reflecting and shit!

Although it is a constant effort to reverse those

behaviours, it really is that easy to become aware of them

to become a better you.

YOU deserve to be the best version of yourself.

Don't Be an 'After' Story

"i urge you to break down that wall of perceived perfection"

Vulnerability was something I struggled with up until recently. I could never find it in myself to go to anyone outside of my Mom with my relationship struggles, insecurities, deepest thoughts and uncertainties. The weird thing was I loved helping people with their problems. I found joy in uplifting them, offering a different approach and educating them if it was something I knew enough about.

Our culture has shifted into everyone wanting to be an 'after story.' It is no longer common to hear about or see someone's struggles, growths and changes especially in this era of social media.

Why don't we want people to see us when we're down? Why is it so hard to be upfront with financial struggles, relationship problems, parenting insecurities etc.?

I can't answer for the majority but personally I would look at myself as weak to discuss my struggles. I didn't want people to know when something was wrong, with the fear of being judged or gossiped about. Thinking about it now, it's stupid because I am very candid regarding my experiences and cannot fathom going back to a time where I kept everything bottled up.

If you are worried about being vulnerable it's time to stop! Here's why:

As Millennials, we have a <u>lack of representation</u> in the everyday world. Social media has conditioned us to always appear perfect *(especially with all the damn filters)*. So when another person comes along that looks up to you and your accomplishments, you *(being the goal)* becomes almost unreachable because your life *looks perfect*.

We all know perfection <u>isn't real</u> but when we are always seeing people happy and successful as shit, we reflect on our own lives wondering what's wrong with me, where do I fit in; because you're not like them. Sounds stupid reading it but I'm sure you've done it.

Here are some of my personal social media vs. reality examples:

1. *Post: a happy baby photo of my son and I*

   - *Comment: So cute, you're such a great Mom!*

   - *Reality: He puked on me 5 seconds before, I haven't slept, already cried twice today from Mom guilt*

2. *Post: photo of myself*

   - *Comment: *heart eyes and flames**

   - *Reality: took about 30 photos, sucked in my stomach, argued with the photo taker (my husband) because I was picking myself apart when he was calling me beautiful*

3. *Post: business update*

- *Comment: look at you go! *fire flame**
- *Reality: this didn't come out of nowhere - it was years in the making, had to get out of my own head and not worry about other people's opinions*

In one of my first truly vulnerable social media posts I experienced first hand the importance of sharing our journeys and realities based on my followers' responses. I kept this same energy going forward.

Step 10: Create your own post/comment/reality example:

Post:

Comment:

Reality:

I urge you to break down that wall of perceived perfection.

Once you are able to be comfortable with being your authentic self, you will see the world flourish around you! You'll build more authentic relationships and will build more confidence overall!

If you've built a business, share your story of struggle and growth. If you're a beauty influencer, share images of you as you regularly are. If you're a motivational speaker, admit that you're not motivated everyday.

Just be a normal human.

It's Just the Beginning

"you read this book for a reason"

I know I threw a lot of shit at you in a very condensed way

but please understand that everything takes time.

The worst thing you can do is attempt to adjust a handful

of things at the same time, because you'll only be left

feeling defeated and overwhelmed. This is why I had you

write down one goal at the beginning of this book.

What was it?

This express guide has provided you with the fundamental and necessary mindset adjustments to dominate that goal and move on to the next. Thinking I'm over exaggerating? Look at all the shit you learned and addressed:

- You were able to clearly define one realistic goal
- You were able to self reflect on your own toxic traits and make the necessary adjustments to lead to a more positive outlook
- You found positivity during a pandemic
- You took the steps to detox your social media
- You failed properly
- You reflected on your personal relationships
- You clearly defined success

- You mentally addressed negative incidences from your childhood and how to change them

- You reflected on your own level of vulnerability

Look at YOU, killin' it!

These were all elements that held me back in the journey that I am still on and overcoming that <u>opened the doors to positivity, self-love and true empowerment.</u>

I may not know you, but <u>I believe in you</u>. Anyone that would pick up a book with a title like this is already amazing in my eyes.

The biggest win though is not answering the questions - **it all comes down to what you do with this information**

and self-reflection. Like I mentioned, I DON'T want this to be just another self-empowerment book that makes you feel good in the moment; and then go back to your everyday bullshit!

You read this book for a reason. You wanted to make the changes and get rid of what was holding you back.

So once again,

Happy New Year, Happy Birthday, it's the first of the month, happy Monday.. whatever day you need it to be to implement what you JUST experienced - it is today, because it is time to

Break Free of the Bullshit!

Acknowledgements

Before I dive into anything I need to thank *YOU* for reading this book, for the follows, likes, comments and shares. Whether you felt you really needed it or were reading out of support, I appreciate the action more than you know! Midway through this process I thought, *"what if no one even picks my book up..?"*

Thank you for proving me wrong.

Now, depending on how you felt about the book, this first group of people that need to be acknowledged are my Advanced Readers. What this means is, if you loved it *THANK YOU* and if you thought it was shitty, here is a list of people to blame *hahaha*: **A.J. Serjue, Adrian Reeves, Aliah Johnson, Cyndi Anker, Debbie Young, Ghazala Knight, Jason Chuck, Joey Sarpong, Jordan Serjue, Josh Burgess, Julie Page and Schenelle Dias.**

I cannot thank this diverse, inspirational, bullshit free group enough for all the support, feedback and for calling me out on my shit and forcing me to dig deeper. Thank you will never be enough but you're all stuck with me for life anyway so I still have time to make it up to you :)

Jacob: Mama always wanted to write a book. I've always been full of ideas but would never execute them. Becoming your Mom gave me the drive, purpose and confidence to take my business to the next step because I finally realized I have what it takes *(thanks to you)* but I also wanted to make you proud. Selfishly, I also wanted you to have something extra to brag about aside from having the coolest Mom in the world haha.

You scribbled all over my book notes, interrupted my writing sessions to play with you and Dada and gave me those much needed hugs when I was feeling defeated - I wouldn't have it any other way. Thank you for inspiring me, this book and for being my everyday reminder to be and do better xo

PS. I don't know how old you'll be when you read this but you better have skipped over all the swear words..

To the one who helped me break free of the majority of the bullshit in my life regardless of how stubborn and annoying I was - my husband, **A.J.:** Thank you for constantly cheering me on, supporting me and believing in me even when I didn't believe in myself. Thank you for motivating me to get back to writing when I'd rather watch my murder documentaries and inspiring me to better organize my time because you do it everyday. You're also my videographer *(the greatest out there)*, photographer, editor, media consultant and a handful of other things! Thank you for making everything look amazing, for making sure I have content, for understanding my visions when I'm not being clear and for staying up late to help me when you have work in the morning! Thank you for being my right hand man not only with this book but in life! We did it babe!

Aliah: There were many moments that you escaped that *'little sister'* role and acted like the older one to get me in check and remind me who I am and what I'm trying to accomplish with this book. Regardless of how busy your life was, thank you for always taking the time to stay updated, give feedback and keep me motivated when I became so overwhelmed *(even though you probably didn't have a choice).* I've also experienced the majority of the bullshit referenced in this book with you by my side so thank you for being my partner in crime even when shit hits the fan.

Mom and Dad: your support and help through the process means the world. Thank you for listening to all my ideas, helping with editing, reviewing contracts, reassuring me when I was unsure and not getting mad about all the swearing and finding out I got caught for plagiarism. I hope I made you guys proud.

Grandpa Young: Thank you for being there without being there. Thank you for pulling me out of those dark holes I often put myself in and reminding me that I am able. Thank you for always cheering me on <3

Debbie Horovitch: From the first time we spoke I knew this was a match made in heaven - I just planned multiple meetings so I looked more professional haha! I cannot thank you enough for making this experience more than amazing. Thank you for your expertise but also for the therapy sessions, the laughs and understanding that I have to change appointments last minute because my son refuses to nap. Cheers to this book and more to come!

My longtime friend, Brother from another Mother and Business Manager - *Joey Sarpong:* Who would have thought two University roommates that were jogging to McDonalds, partying all night when we had 8AM classes and living like we had no responsibilities would be at this point in life now haha! Thank you for not only being an amazing friend but believing in my business, creating that much needed structure for growth and making sure I don't get lost in the sauce. So thankful to have you on my team personally and professionally!

Ryan Pornasdoro: Right when the 'adulting' began for me you were there! Now, I know that wasn't the intention -

you just happened to work beside a girl that talked so much but I couldn't be more thankful for the relationship we've built over the years haha! Thank you for being there when my business was just an idea. I told you WHEN I get an opportunity to make shit happen I want you a part of it in any way possible so the fact that you created and absolutely killed all visuals of this book means the world to me! Thank you isn't enough but know this is just the beginning *fire flames*!

Jacobs Creek - Moscato: My go to for the times I needed to take a break from writing and when I celebrated next steps - thank you!

Penni Lafleur: I could have made an entire chapter about our experience together! I remember after one of our meetings I asked if there was someone I could email about how amazing you are - you never gave me that contact because this is more than a job for you, you actually care. I cannot express how thankful I am to have met you and how monumental your presence is in my life to bring me to the point I'm at now. I really feel like thank you isn't enough but thank you x1000000! Any student that gets to work with you is lucky beyond words!

Cyndi Anker, Ghazala Knight, Marlena Mensour and Schenelle Dias: Aside from my family (*although you are family*), you ladies were there from the beginning - before the book and before the business if not daily, at least weekly. Thank you! Thank you for not only inspiring me with your own accomplishments but for motivating me with mine. Thanks for all the feedback, for calling me out on my shit, for celebrating the milestones and for

helping me with the things I needed and/or didn't know I

needed. I'm not sure how I got so lucky to have you all in

my circle but thankful doesn't even begin to describe it.

We're all winning! Love you!

And finally

to **those who inspired it, but will never read it.** Thank you

for the good and the bad.

SPEAKER | AUTHOR | FOUNDER Of PaigeIofSome

PAIGE JOHNSON-SERJUE

CHANGING THE NARRATIVE BY STARTING THE CONVERSATION

SIGNATURE TOPICS
Maternal Representation
Normalizing Failure
Power of Building Self Up
Goal Setting
Breaking the Cycle
+ More

SPECIALTIES
Guest Speaker
Host
Keynote Speaker
Panelist
Workshop Facilitator

LET'S KEEP IN TOUCH!
Instagram: PaigeIofSome
Facebook: PaigeIofSome
Website: breakthenarrative.com

"WHETHER YOU THINK
YOU CAN OR YOU
CAN'T, YOU'RE RIGHT"
- HENRY FORD

I'LL SHOW YOU THAT
YOU CAN AND YOU WILL

FOR BOOKING INFORMATION
CONTACT:
paigeIofsome@outlook.com

TALK TO YOU SOON !

ORDER
COPIES OF

break free of the bullsh*t
A Millennial Empowerment Guide

COPIES	PRICE ($CAD)
1-4	$24.99
5-49	$22.00
50-99	$18.00
100-499	$14.00
500+	$10.00

PLEASE ALLOW MINIMUM OF
TWO WEEKS TO FULFILL ORDER

PLEASE EMAIL:

paige1ofsome@outlook.com

TO PLACE YOUR ORDER

THANK YOU

About the Author

Paige is a burger loving, wine indulging cool Mom that uses her *'gift of gab'* aka motivational speaking platform to empower the millennial generation both personally and professionally.

She's unfiltered but compassionate and genuinely gives a shit about changing the narrative surrounding this generation.

Looking for consistent empowerment, a good laugh and a dose of inspiration? Visit the below:

https://breakfreeofthebsbook.com
@paige1ofsome - Instagram URL:
https://www.instagram.com/paige1ofsome/?hl=en
Youtube -
https://www.youtube.com/channel/UC8QRMEoGvcr4OV_dhe
Zvktg

You can also contact her directly:
paige1ofsome@outlook.com

Made in the USA
Coppell, TX
22 December 2020